# Double Stop Musings for Cello

book three    by Cassia Harvey

CHP162

©2005 by C. Harvey Publications  All Rights Reserved.

www.charveypublications.com - print books
www.learnstrings.com - PDF downloadable books
www.harveystringarrangements.com - chamber music

# 1

Cassia Harvey

Double Stop Musings for Cello, Book Three

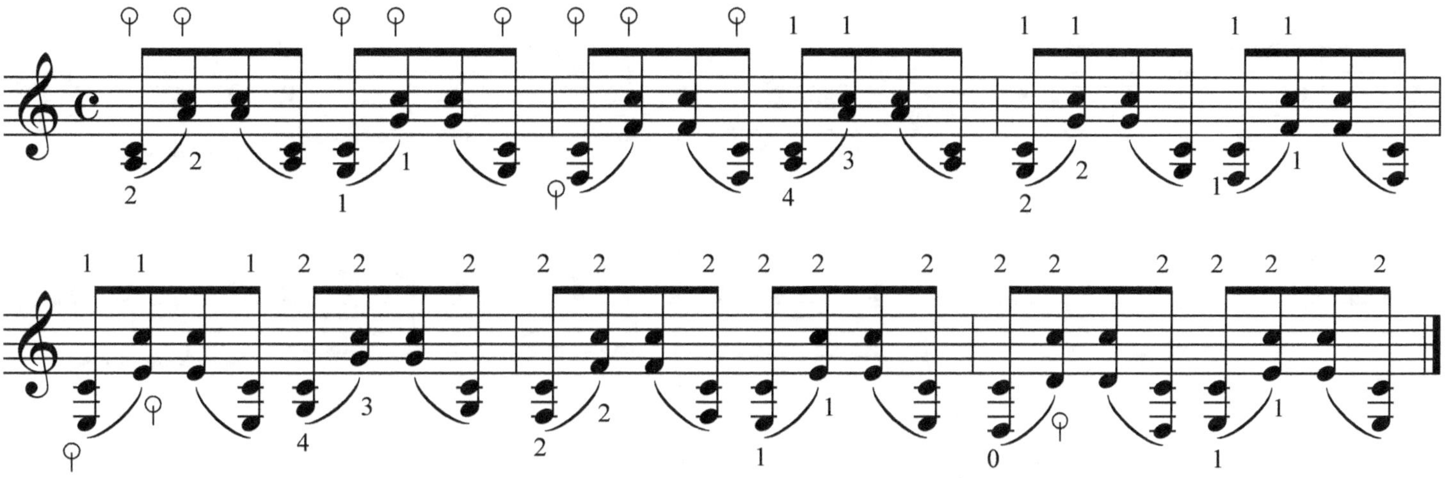

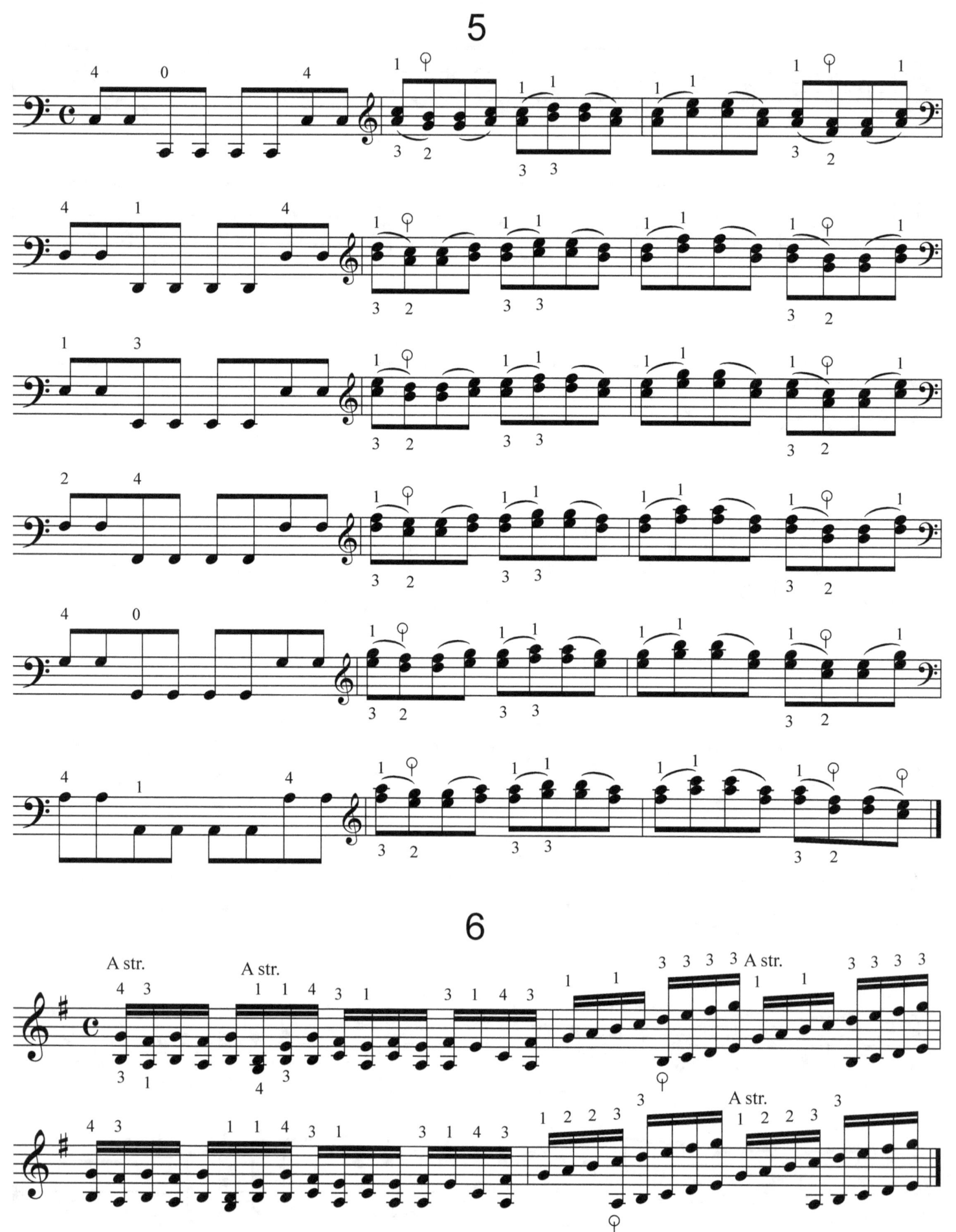

Double Stop Musings for Cello, Book Three

# 9

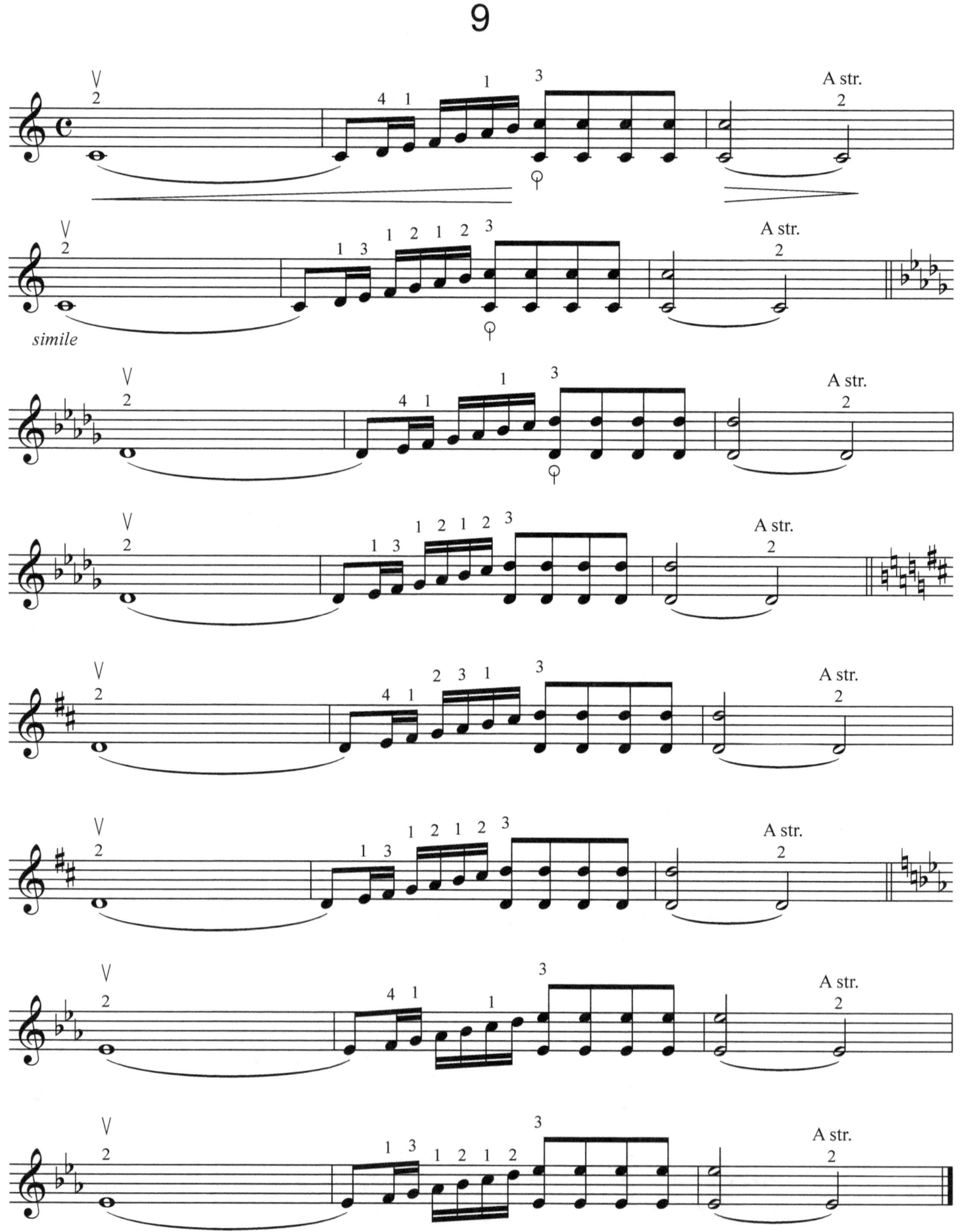

Double Stop Musings for Cello, Book Three

# 14

Double Stop Musings for Cello, Book Three

Double Stop Musings for Cello, Book Three                                    13

©2006 C. Harvey Publications All Rights Reserved.

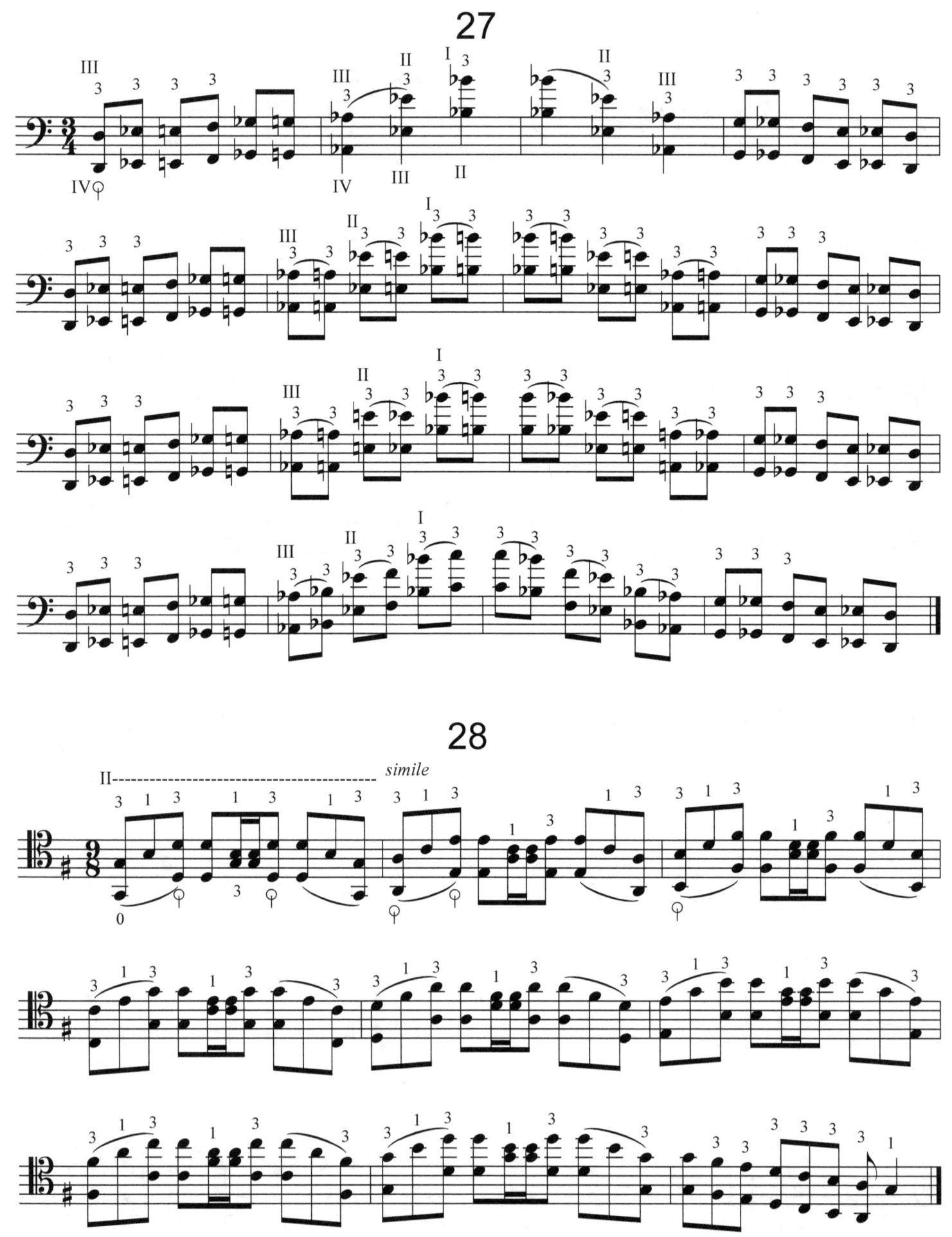

Double Stop Musings for Cello, Book Three

## 29

©2006 C. Harvey Publications All Rights Reserved.

# 30

# 32

# 33

Double Stop Musings for Cello, Book Three

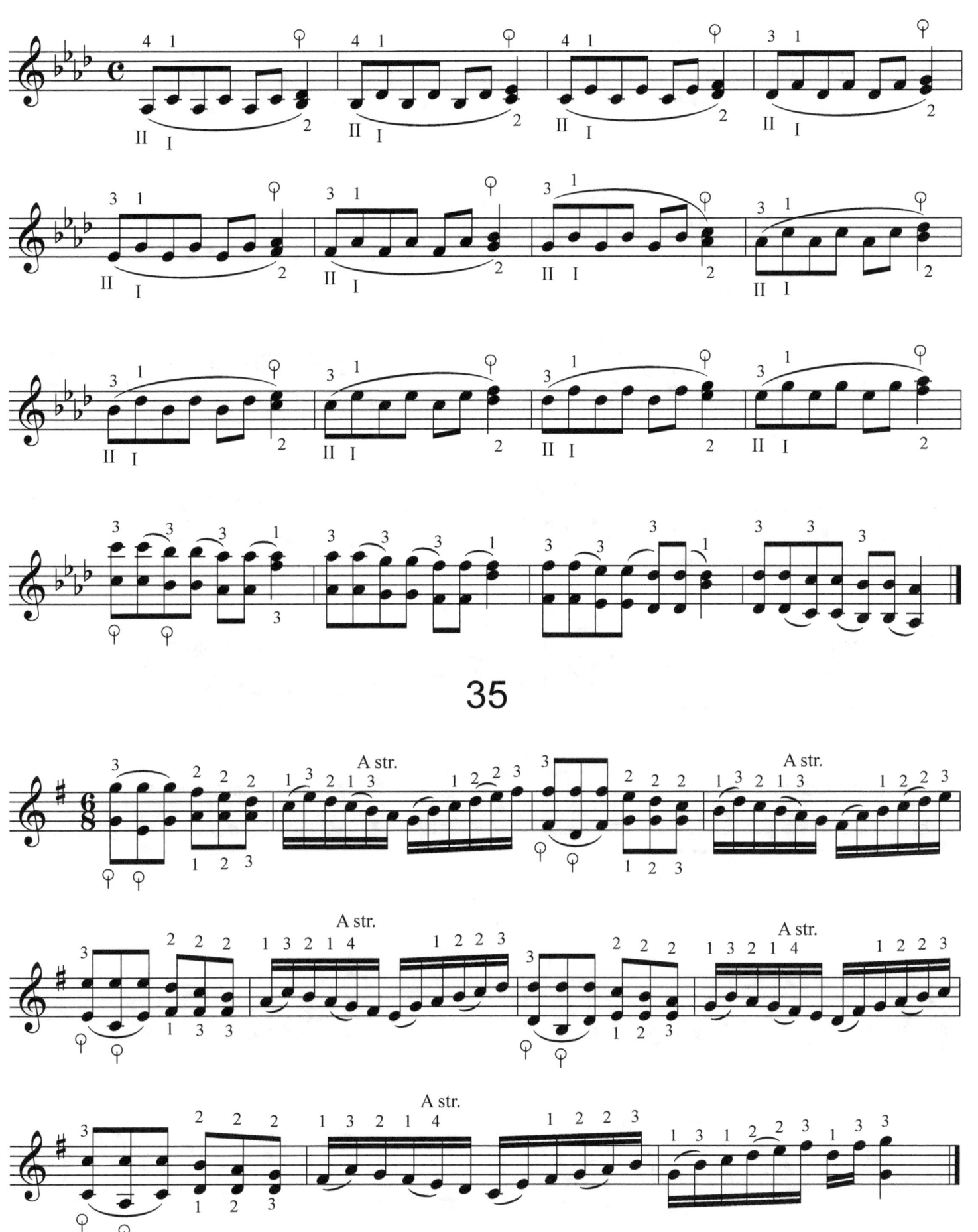

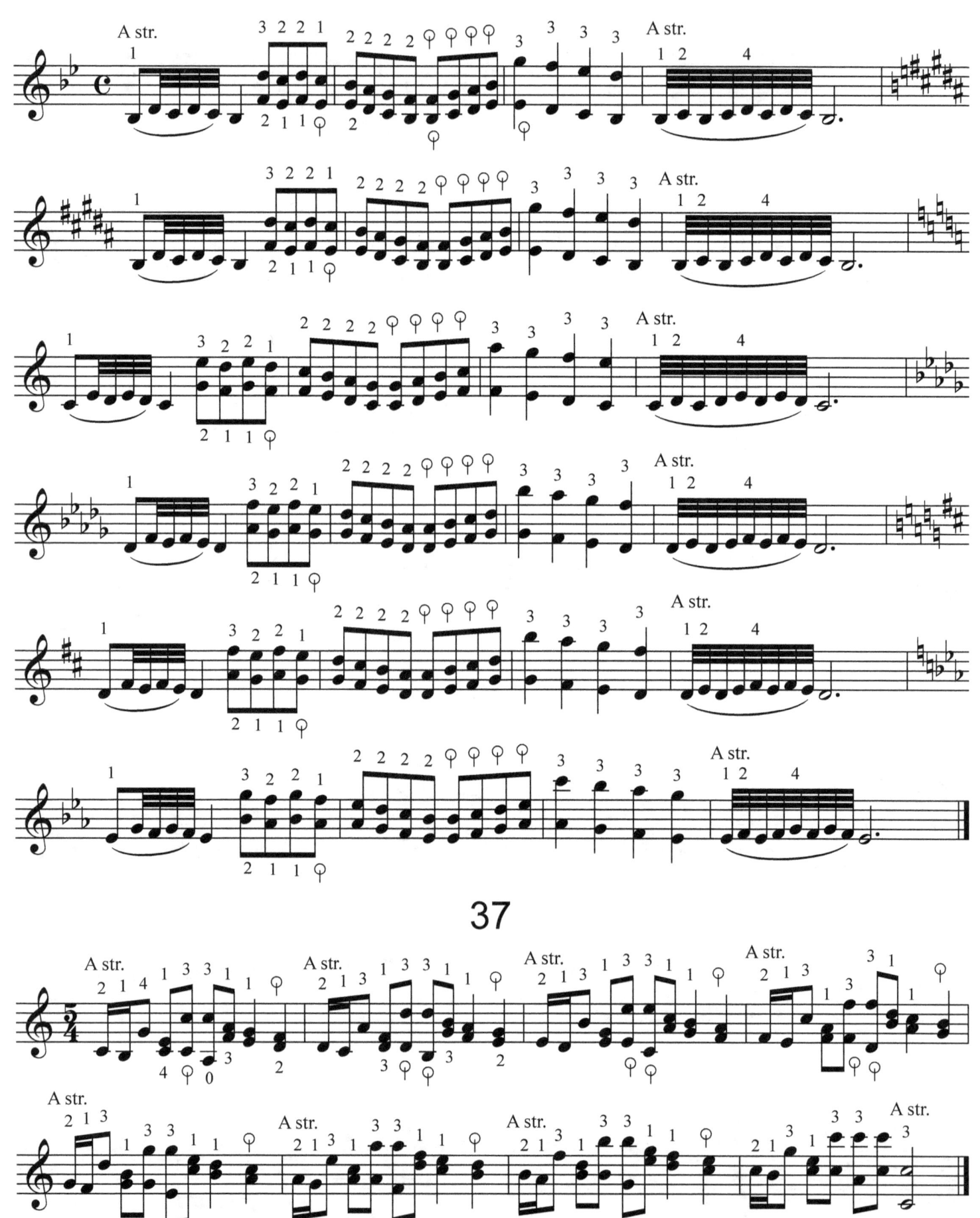

Double Stop Musings for Cello, Book Three

23

# 40

Double Stop Musings for Cello, Book Three

Double Stop Musings for Cello, Book Three

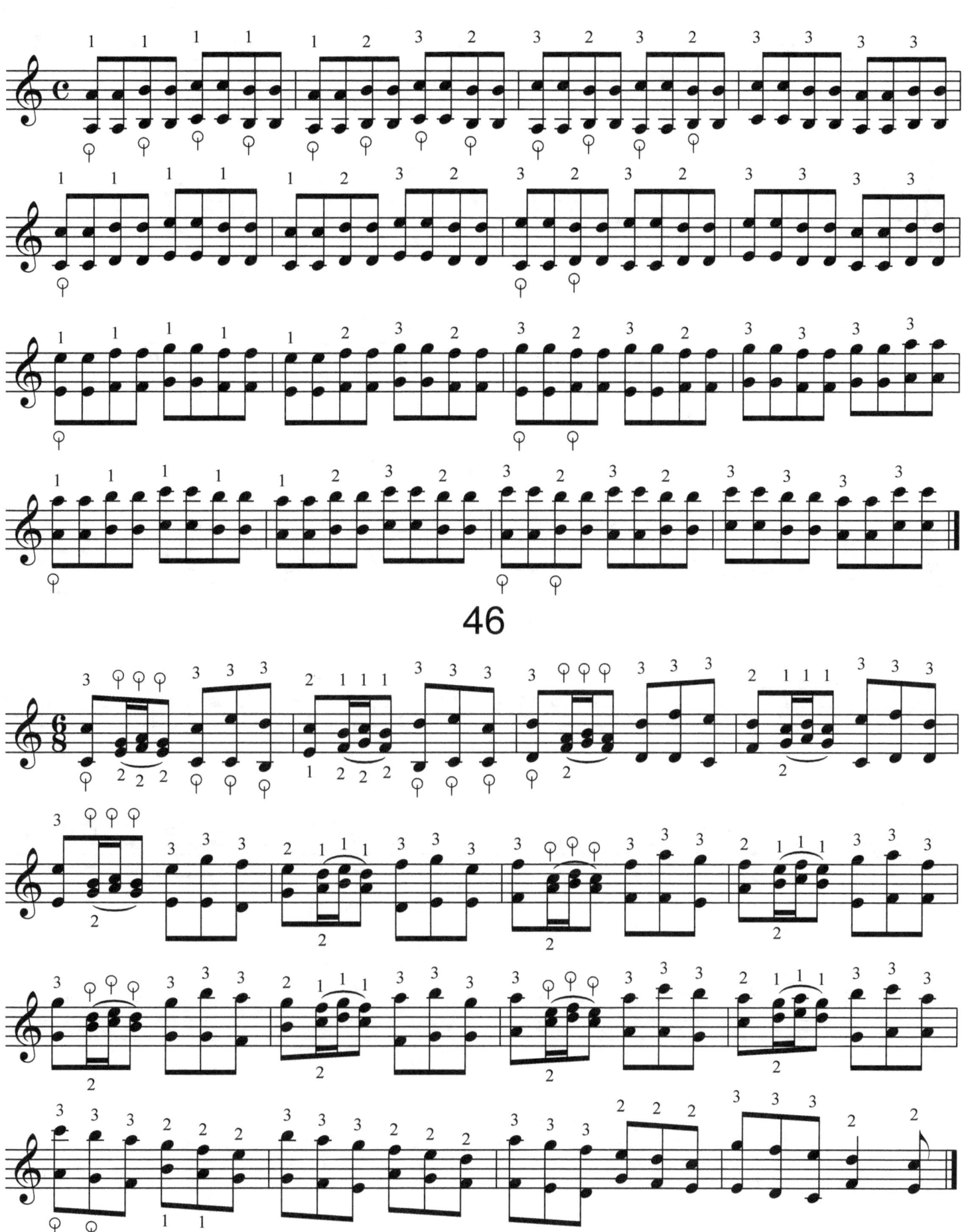

Double Stop Musings for Cello, Book Three

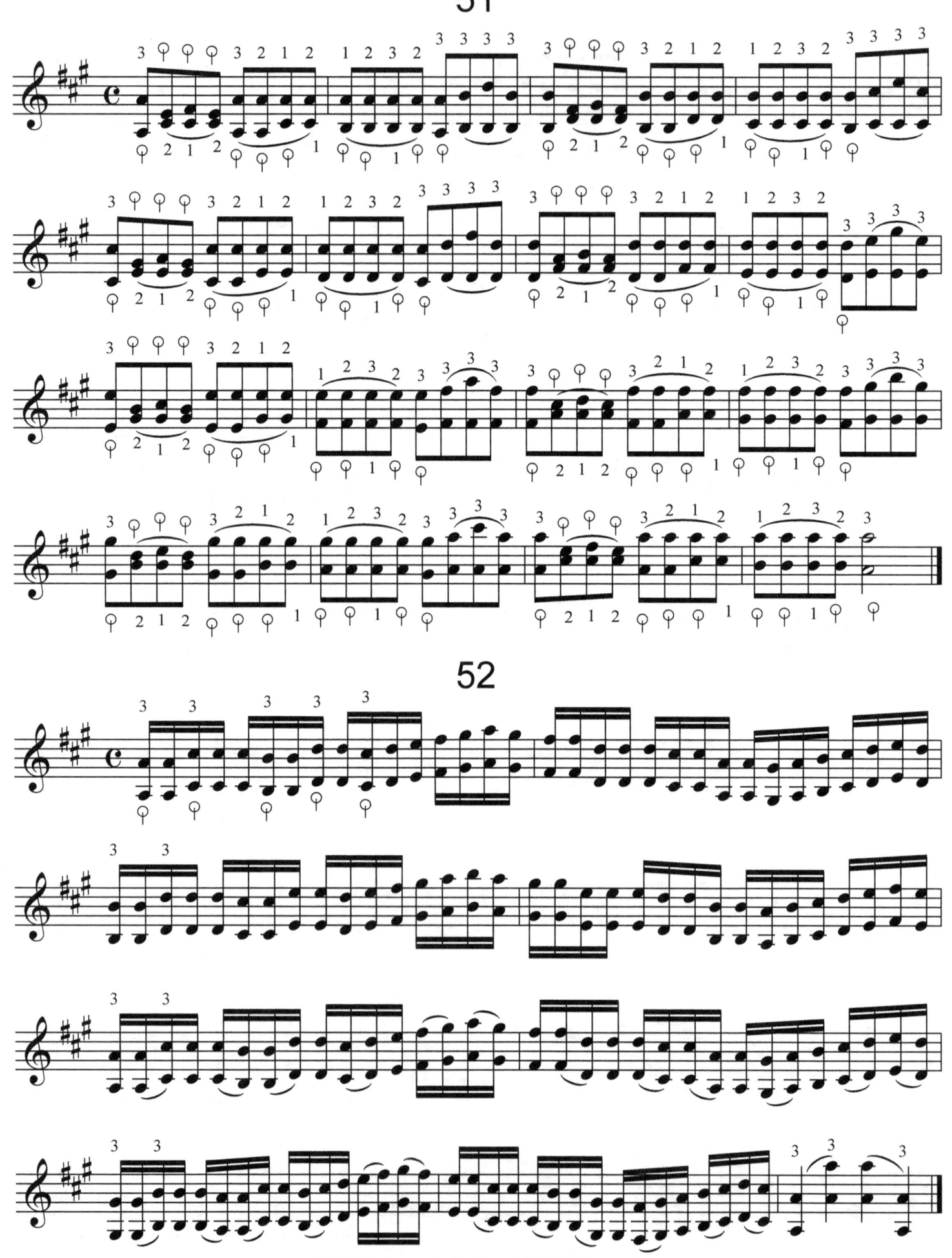

Double Stop Musings for Cello, Book Three

## 53

©2006 C. Harvey Publications All Rights Reserved.